ISBN 978-1-334-01148-1
PIBN 10120243

THE

FIRST BOOK

OF

NAPOLEON,

THE

TYRANT OF THE EARTH:

WRITTEN

IN THE 5813th YEAR OF THE WORLD, AND
1809th YEAR OF THE CHRISTIAN ERA,

BY

ELIAKIM THE SCRIBE,

A DESCENDANT OF A MODERN BRANCH OF THE TRIBE
OF LEVI; A RABBI EDUCATED IN THE CHRISTIAN
SCHOOLS OF THE SONS OF THE PROPHETS.

"Lo, and behold! a mean-born stranger shall come from afar; and ye shall pay obeisance
"unto him, and fear him, and lick the dust under his feet, and tremble under his
"crown, which unto you shall be a crown of iron."
BOOK OF NAPOLEON, Chap. II. verse 14.

LONDON:

SOLD BY LONGMAN, HURST, REES, & ORME,
AND J. J. STOCKDALE, PALL-MALL; P. HILL, EDINBURGH;
AND M. KEENE, DUBLIN.
1809.

14 0.1

N

ELIAKIM'S

ADDRESS TO HIS READERS.

———

CHARITABLE and GENTLE READER! to thee
the Author of this Book has little to say, thy
attributes being the godlike virtues of meekness
and charity.

PIOUS and RELIGIOUS READER! let not thy
feelings be offended, and withhold thy censure,
until thou shalt find in these pages a single sen-
timent inconsistent with the spirit and principles of that holy religion which thou profess-
est; and condemn not the feebly imitative manner of writing therein occasionally employed,
until thou canst point out a language more
impressive, or more appropriate, than that in
imitation whereof these chapters are framed.

READERS IN GENERAL! take warning from
the awful examples, and profit by the whole-

some admonitions therein contained, and be-
lieve that they are truly intended for your good
and welfare.

NAPOLEON! if, peradventure, this little volume should ever reach thee, may its truths sink
deep into thine heart, and remember in the midst
of the torrents of blood thy guilty ambition is shed-
ding, and the ruin and desolation it is spreading
far and wide, that thou art a mortal man ; and
one day, perhaps ere long, thy soul shall be
required of thee, and an account of all thy deeds,
by that omnipotent, unerring, and upright Being, who, as he made and governeth, so in
like manner shall he judge the world.

KING OF THE ALBIONS! of whom mention
is made in these pages, be assured, that the ef-
fusions of loyalty to thy person, and admiration
of thy virtues, which they contain, are those not
of the author only, but of a brave, affectionate,
and dutiful people.

ELIAKIM.

CONTENTS

OF

THE FIRST BOOK OF NAPOLEON.

—————

CHAP. I.

CHAP. II.

CHAP. III.

CONTENTS.

CHAP. VII.

CHAP. VIII.

CHAP. IX.

CHAP. X.

CHAP. XI.

CHAP. XII.

CHAP. XIII.

CHAP. XIV.

ERRATA.

Chap.   II.   verse 8,   *for* but *read* except.
———   III.   ——— 17,   — backs — ruins.
———   IV.   ——— 18,   — ways — designs.
———   IX.   ——— 28,   — overthrow none — overthrown one.
———   XII.   ——— 4,   — traiterous — traitorous.
———   XIII. ——— 37,   — infalliably — infallibly.

NAPOLEON

THE TYRANT.

BOOK I.

CHAP. I.

AND behold it came to pass, in these latter days, that an evil spirit arose on the face of the earth, and greatly troubled the sons of men.

2

And this spirit seized upon, and spread amongst the people who dwell in the land of Gaul.

3

Now, in this people the fear of the Lord had not been for many generations, and they had become a corrupt and perverse people; and their chief priests, and the nobles of the land, and the learned men thereof, had become wicked in the imaginations of their hearts, and in the practices of their lives.

4

And the evil spirit went abroad amongst the people, and they raged like unto the heathen, and they rose up against their lawful king, and slew him, and his queen also, and the prince their son; yea, verily, with a cruel and bloody death.

5

And they moreover smote, with mighty wrath, the king's guards, and banished the priests, and nobles of the land, and seized upon, and took unto themselves, their inheritances, their gold and silver, corn and oil, and whatsoever belonged unto them.

6

Now it came to pass, that the nation of the Gauls continued to be sorely troubled and vexed, and the evil spirit whispered unto the people, even unto the meanest and vilest thereof, that all men being born equal, were free to act, each one according to the imaginations and devices of his own heart, without the fear of God, or the controul of the lawful rulers of the land.

7

And lo! this foolish and wicked counsel of evil designing men, being seemly, and well-pleasing in the sight of the multitude, they raged furiously against all principalities and powers; and having slain the good king whom the Lord had appointed to rule over them, and to administer justice unto them; they moreover sought to overthrow and destroy the kings and rulers over the other nations of the earth, and made war upon them; and stirred up the people of those nations in like manner to wage war against the lawful rulers of the lands, wherein they had been appointed to dwell.

8

Now, it so happened, that the evil spirit stirred up every one to seek his own exaltation, by humbling and debasing those whom GOD had made superior to him, in mind, body, and estate.

9

And while this spirit raged in Gaul, the curse of GOD was upon the land, and bloodshed, murder, and rapine, and all manner of blasphemy, wickedness, and uncleanness, prevailed amongst the people thereof.

10

And they not only despised the commandments of the LORD, but also blasphemed the name of the only true and living GOD, and they made idols and false gods to themselves, and fell down and worshipped them.

11

And lo. and behold, the chief idol, which this wicked and perverse people set up and worshipped, was like unto a beast, although made somewhat after the image of a man.

12

And out of the head of the beast there arose three horns, and upon each of the horns there were written these words, SEDITION, PRIVY CONSPIRACY, and REBELLION; and on the forehead of the beast, and under the horns, there were written, in letters of blood, the words T.REASONS and CRIMES.

13

And from the eyes of the beast there proceeded flashes of devouring fire, and its jaws and throat were like unto the mouth of hell, and from its tongue there issued cursings and blasphemings.

14

And upon the breast of the beast, there were written these words, IRRELIGION, INFIDELITY, and TUMULT.

15

And in its right hand, it held an emblem of fire and sword, and in its left, an emblem of rapine and murder.

16

And upon the feet of the beast, there were brazen sandals, like unto those worn by men, and upon the sandal of the right foot, there was engraven, in letters of brass, TERROR and DISMAY; and upon the sandal of the left foot, BLOOD and FAMINE, signifying, that wheresoever the beast established itself, or trode, those direful evils would afflict the land.

17

And behold, the name of the idol was called LICENTIOUSNESS.

18

And lo ! a loud and warning voice, proceeding as it were from the heavens on high, was heard upon the earth beneath, saying, " Beware, O man, of the exceeding great vileness and abominations of the beast or idol herein described, for upon the followers and worshippers thereof, there shall descend justice, and divers and direful judgments."

CHAP. II.

1. The evil spirit increaseth.—2. The corrupt tree, and its fruits.—3. It is a cumberer of the ground, and doth not prosper therein : but is cast down, and destroyed.

AND the evil spirit continued to spread itself amongst the nations of the earth, and they were sorely afflicted, and troubled therewith.

2

And the idolatry of the beast in like manner prevailed among the sons of men, and it pleased the LORD to deliver the worshippers thereof into the hands of the Gauls.

3

Now the Gauls continued to rage as heretofore, with mighty ire, and waged war against all nations, people, and languages.

4

And the kings and rulers of the earth, beheld the raging of the storm, and combined together to quell the fury thereof.

5

But the power of the evil spirit, and of the multitude which it moved, was mighty great, and from amongst them there arose valiant captains, and men of war, and they overthrew those that waged war against them.

6

And lo! the tillers of the ground, and the labourers thereof, together with mechanics, artificers, and all manner of handicraftmen, left their sundry and peaceful occupations, and became lawmakers and lawgivers, and sought to rule over their superiors.

7

Now, it had pleased the LORD to darken the

understandings of those foolish men ; for they vainly imagined, that laws and institutions may be forthwith made, like unto things of cunning device, or built in a season, or by models, like unto earthly habitations ; whereas, they grow naturally and gradually after the manner of trees, and, like them, require to be trained and pruned by the wary hand of age and time.

8

Now, as good and wholesome laws and institutions, or, as they are called in these latter days, good constitutions, after the manner of trees, do not take root and grow but in good soils, and where they are well watered and sheltered ; so, in like manner, as is known unto all husbandmen, the tree that springeth and flourisheth in one, and a good soil, decayeth and dieth in another, or bad soil.

9

As the dew of heaven, and the sun-beams thereof, water and cherish the earthly tree, so also, do the spirits of the departed patriots of a land, and the blood of the warriors thereof, foster and support the political tree, or constitution of the state.

10

But the Gauls were altogether a wicked and perverse people, and the tree which they had planted in the midst of them was a blasted tree, and lo and behold, it brought forth nothing but bad and forbidden fruit, and all manner of unrighteousness, such as pertaineth unto the idol of whom it is before-written, and whom they, in the foolish imaginations of their hearts, had vainly worshipped.

11

And this evil tree was planted in many and divers places; but the leaves and branches thereof decayed, and were blasted, and its roots rotted; because the sap which was in the tree, was poison, and all those who tasted of its fruit perished thereby; yea, even with a cruel and bloody death.

12

And behold the tree partook of the nature of the beast, of which it is before-written; for it had sprung from the rottenness and corruption thereof.

13

And when the LORD looked down from heaven, and beheld the perverse wickedness of the Gauls, he said, yea, verily, I will punish this people for the wickedness of their ways.

14

So the LORD spake by his prophets, and said unto the people of Gaul, O foolish people, ye have cast down and slain, with a cruel and igno- minious death, the king whom I had appointed to rule over you, and whose fathers had reigned in the land for many generations; and ye have destroyed all principalities and powers, and have despised all holy things, and have imagi- ned vain and wicked conceits, and have more- over troubled the peace of the world, and sworn enmity to the kings and rulers of the earth; but I will punish you, O people, for these evil doings; and lo and behold, a mean born stran- ger shall come from afar, and ye shall pay obei- sance to him, and fear him, and lick the dust under his feet, and tremble under his crown, which, unto you, shall be a crown of iron.

15

And lo! the prophecy of the LORD was ful- filled, as will be made manifest from what is hereafter written in this book.

CHAP. III.

1. *The Birth-place of the Tyrant Napoleon.—2. He pro_
fesseth himself to be a worshipper of the idol.—3. He
goeth into the land of Egypt, wageth war, and sojour_
neth for some time there.—4. He threateneth Pales_
tine and Jerusalem.—5. He returneth suddenly from
thence, and destroyeth the first Idol, and putteth him_
self at the head of the armies of the Gauls.—6. He be_
cometh a mighty Conqueror, powerful in war, and over_
whelmeth many of the kings and princes of the earth.
—7. He is a punishment unto the nations for the
wickedness of their ways.—8. The oppressed cry aloud
unto the LORD for relief from the oppressor; but for
a season he listeneth not unto them, and hardeneth
the Tyrant's heart, because of the perverse wickedness
of the people.*

Now, in the land called Corsica, which is an
island in the sea, there was a man born, and his
name was NAPOLEON.

2

And this man, though small in stature, was
nevertheless vast in spirit, and he not only con_
ceived unto himself, great and marvellous de_

signs, but was moreover wicked, and cunning in council, mighty in deeds, and powerful in war.

3

And he professed himself to be a true worshipper of the idol, and yet he hated the idol in his heart, and had made unto himself another idol, of the nature, whereof it is hereafter written.

4

And he declared himself to be an enemy unto all principalities and powers, and the friend of freedom and equality amongst the sons of men, and he was appointed Captain over the armies of the worshippers of the idol.

5

And he commanded the hosts thereof, and went forth against the lawful rulers of the earth, and overthrew them, together with the mighty high priest, who for many generations had commanded the fear and veneration of men.

6

And lo this man went into the land of Egypt, with many ships and a mighty army; and having conquered the inhabitants thereof, he proceeded against Palestine, and threatened the city of Jerusalem.

7

O Jerusalem, Jerusalem, how are the mighty fallen, and how nearly hadst thou been conquered, yet 'a second time, by the arm of an infidel.

8

But behold the progress of this man, in the land of Egypt, was stopped by a captain of the navy of good King Albanus, the King of the Albions, the history of whom is herein after written.

9.

Now, this man Napoleon, after sojourning for many days in the land of Egypt, suddenly took his departure from thence, and returned unto the country of the Gauls, and overthrew like a whirlwind the rulers thereof, and put himself at the head of the armies of the multitude, and declared himself to be the governor of the nation, which he began to rule with a rod of iron.

10.

And this man being a mighty man of war,

and a great captain, put himself at the head of the hosts of the Gauls, and thirsted for glory, dominion, and power.

11.

And he waged war against the surrounding nations, and overthrew one people after another.

12.

And his hosts were in number like unto the sands of the sea, and in power to the thunders of the skies; for his deeds resembled in quickness the lightning of heaven, and in might they were likened unto the thunderbolts thereof.

13.

And lo, the people of Gaul forgot their former idol, which is described in the beginning of this book, and fell down and worshipped this strange and new idol, the nature whereof differed from the former in manner and in kind.

14.

For upon the crown of this idol, which being a man, was altogether after the likeness thereof, there were written Dominion, Principalities, and Power; and under the crown, which was an iron crown, and on the

forehead of the man there was written AMBI-
TION ; and on his breastplate there were also
written, COUNSEL, PROMPTITUDE, and DE-
CEIT.

15.

And the man Napoleon held in his right
hand a sword of steel, whereon were engraven
DEATH, VICTORY, and CONQUEST, and in his
left a roll of parchment, and in the roll was
written the DOMINION of the WORLD, and under the same the names of the nations which
he had conquered, yea all people within the
reach of his power.

16.

And on the sandal of his right foot there was
engraven, in letters of brass, OPPRESSION, and
on that of his left, SLAVERY.

17.

And his throne, which reached unto the
clouds, was raised on the backs of fallen nations,
once great and glorious, but now prostrate and
humbled in the dust.

18.

For he had overthrown, like a whirlwind,
and in the twinkling of an eye, the armies of

many of the kings and rulers of the nations of
the earth ; because they had become vile and
polluted in all manner of sinful corruption, and
would not be warned by the voice of wisdom,
and combine firmly together, nor be true and
faithful one to another ; but listened to the sug-
gestions of the evil spirit and of the idol, which
had darkened their understandings, and prepared them for downfal and ruin.

19.

Now, the sway of this man pervaded many
lands, and many of the kings and princes of the
earth were made tributary to him, and the nations thereof groaned under his feet.

20.

And he now compelled the tillers of the
ground, and the labourers thereof, and the husbandmen, and handicraftmen, who, under the
first idol, had met together to commune concerning superiorities and powers, and to make
laws unto themselves, to leave their peaceful
homes, their wives, children, and kindred, and
their lawful occupations, and to go into distant
lands, and there endure cold and hunger, and
suffer long marches, and mix in direful and

bloody battles, all to fill up the measure of this man's boundless ambition.

21

And it pleased the LORD, as a punishment for the wickedness and perverseness of the people, to deliver into the hands of this man the dominion over many lands, that they might be ruled as with a rod of iron, and chastened for the iniquity and wickedness of their ways, and brought back from the paths of sin and licentiousness, and the idolatry of the beast, to those of justice, moderation, and truth, and the fear of the only true and living GOD.

22

And the people of the land of Gaul, and all the nations whom it had pleased the LORD to deliver into the hands of this strange man, groaned heavily, and cried unto the LORD in their hearts for freedom, forgiveness, and mercy.

23

But having forgot and despised the LORD their GOD, in the pride and wickedness of their hearts, he left them to reap the fruits of their evil ways, and for a season listened not unto them in their sufferings and distress.

24

Now, behold, all the nations within the reach of this man Napoleon, groaned under the dominion of his power, and were sore afflicted in mind, body, and estate, for he ruled over them with a sceptre of iron.

CHAP. IV.

Character of Napoleon.

1

THE wise man in scripture hath said, that " the fear of the Lord is the beginning of knowledge ;" but it is moreover the very perfection and consummation of wisdom.

2

True, O Napoleon, thy perceptions are quick, thy promptitude and execution great, thy deceit and effrontery unexampled, and thy skill and courage in war undeniable; but thou hast failed in giving proofs of that soundness and solidity of judgment, that greatness, goodness, and nobleness of mind, which are the peculiar attributes of true wisdom and genuine dignity.

3

Hence, thou hast dazzled mankind by the brilliancy of thy deeds, and by rearing on a sudden, a vast and splendid fabric; but its foundation is on the sandy basis of force and terror, and when the reason, courage, and reflection of the nations thou hast conquered, shall emerge from the veil thou hast cast over them, the foundation of the fabric thou hast raised shall be undermined, and swept away by the returning current of rational and regenerated liberty.

4

Whereas, hadst thou been a man of great wisdom and of sound understanding, thou mightest have erected upon the rock of genuine freedom, a great edifice of solid dimensions, which was not likely to have been moved from its foundation, and which thou and thy descendants might have in-

habited in peace and gladness for many generations.

5

But thou art the child of a boundless ambition, and the sport of an ungovernable passion,
which hurrieth the inheritor thereof to ruin and
destruction.

6

As thou hast not given proofs of sound and
solid judgment and understanding in the things
thou hast done, neither hast thou displayed any
of those noble qualities of the heart, which distinguished the brave warriors and great con-
querors of ancient times.

7

Thou art of hasty and fiery temper, cruel
and vindictive, insolent, not compassionate, towards a conquered foe.

8

Thy history doth not say, that thou hast ever
consoled the unfortunate, dried up the tear of
sorrow, or made the mournful eye to sparkle
with gladness.

9

Moreover, well has it been for thee, that, in

the times in which thou hast lived, few of the
kings on the thrones of the surrounding nations
have possessed the talents, or inherited the mar-
tial fire and daring spirits of their ancestors.

10

Nor hast thou been less remarkable for the
numerous victories thou hast gained, than for
the consequences thy art and cunning have en-
abled thee to derive from them.

11

Neither, O Napoleon, thou strange and
wicked man, art thou of any manner of religion:
but contrariwise, an infidel, scoffer, and blasphemer.

12

Didst not thou commence the career of thy
depravity, by blasphemously declaring thyself,
in common with the Gauls, an unbeliever in the
only true and living God, and in the immortality of the soul?

13

Thereafter, at Rome, didst not thou impiously swear on the Holy Evangelists, and bow the
knee to JESUS of Nazareth, the Saviour of the

B 3

World, in whom thou hypocritically professedst thyself to be a sincere Believer ?

14

In the Holy Land, again, nay almost in the very precincts of Jerusalem, and in the places where the Saviour taught and suffered, didst not thou kiss the Koran, and declare Mahomet to be the only true Prophet of God ?

15

Whilst these things were doing, O Heavens, where were thy thunders ?

16

Earth, how came it that thou didst not open thy jaws, and swallow him up ?

17

Ye rocks and ye mountains, why did not ye fall upon and overwhelm him ?

18

Was it because the ways of Providence were not fulfilled with this man on Earth, and that he might be reserved as an instrument of punishment for the wickedness of those nations who should have the impiety to enlist and marshal themselves under the banners of an Infidel, Scoffer, and Blasphemer ?

19

That he might carry into the several lands
of those who were seduced by his cunning deceits, and who were like unto himself impious
and profane, fire and sword, murder, famine,
pestilence and divers evils and diseases?

20

As thy days, O Napoleon, are full of evil
doings, so in like manner are they full of won-
ders; but thy days are quickly passing away,
and the hand of death is stretching itself forth
apace towards thee, and at its sable touch, thy
turbulent and fiery clay shall moulder into
cold and silent dust.

21

As for thy soul, it is in the hand of a Great
and Just God, the giver thereof, nor dare mortal scan its final doom.

22

Nevertheless, history will be full of thy won-
der-working days; and future generations shall
marvel and shudder at the recital of thy daring,
impious, and horrible deeds.

CHAP. V.

1. Description of the Land of Albion, and of the good King that reigneth over the same.—2. His Throne.— 3. Description also of the Tree which had grown and flourished in this Land, for many generations, and of the goodly fruits thereof.

AND it came to pass in those days, that there were a people who dwelt in a land called Albion, which is an island in the sea, and over-against the coast of the land of Gaul.

2

And lo, and behold, deep and mighty waters encompass the land of Albion as with a shield, and the people who dwell therein.

3

Now it had pleased the Lord, not to deliver this people into the hands of the Gauls, nor to put them under the yoke of the tyrant of the earth.

4

And over this people there had reigned for many days and years a good king, who feared the Lord and kept his commandments, and who walked uprightly before the Lord his God.

5

And it had pleased the Lord to bless this good king, and the people over whom he had been appointed to reign, in gentleness and mercy.

6

And the Lord had given unto him many sons and daughters, and a valiant, loving, and faithful people.

7

And the people never ceased shouting aloud all day long, " O king, live for ever !"

8

And this good king was called Albanus, which was also the name of his forefathers, who had reigned in the old times before him.

9

And behold on the crown of the king, which was a golden crown, and set round with precious stones, there were written, MODERATION and MERCY.

10

JUSTICE and TRUTH shone in his counte-

nance ; and from his heart proceeded RELIGION,
PIETY, and DEVOTION.

11

In his right hand he held a sword, whereon
was written DEFENCE, and in his left hand
he held a trident, whereon were engraven in letters of GOLD, these words, " THE DOMINION
" OF THE SEA ;" for it had pleased the LORD
to commit unto him the Sovereignty of the
ocean.

12

And under his throne there were two foot-
stools of GOLD, and on the one foot-stool,
there were engraven FREEDOM and SECU-
RITY, and on the other WEALTH and HAP-
PINESS, signifying, that wheresoever the power
and Dominion of this good king prevailed, these
blessings would fall to the lot of the happy
land.

13.

And in the land of Albion, there grew and
flourished, in peace and happiness, that Tree,
which the other nations of the world had been
foolishly endeavouring to plant and rear, amidst
ruin and desolation, and in seas of blood.

14

And this tree, which was of the nature of an oak, had been planted for many ages, and had fixed its root in the very centre of the land.

15

Now, it had become a fair, beautiful, and mighty tree, and its trunk was like unto a rock, in thickness and solidity, and its branches, which reached even unto the clouds, extended to the remotest corners of the land.

16

And the blessing of God was upon the tree, and whosoever took shelter under its branches, and its leaves, found the shade thereof, safe, cool, and peaceful.

17

And the sap and fruit of the tree were good and nourishing, and not poisonous like unto the sap of that evil tree, which had been planted by the hands of the ungodly in other lands; but which had perished with their ways.

18

Now the root of this fair tree, which struck deep into the land, was cherished and enriched with the blood, and warmed with the ashes of the brave and good men, the forefathers of the Albions, who had either lived in its support, or died in its defence.

19

And the trunk of the tree, which meaneth the constitution of the state, representeth the whole nation, or people of the land.

20

And from the trunk of the tree, there springeth and divergeth four mighty branches.

21

And the first branch is called ROYAL, because it representeth the descent and race of the kings of the land.

22

And the second is called HOLY, because it representeth the church and priesthood of the land.

23

And the third is called NOBLE, because it denoteth the descent and race of the nobles of the land.

24

And the fourth and last branch, denoteth the representatives, or counsellors of the people.

25

And from each of these four great branches, there issue others, and the fruit which
is produced by the tree is emblematical of religion and piety, kingly greatness and goodness, nobleness of birth and deed, freedom, o-
bedience to the laws, security, wealth, and happiness.

26

Now, behold these four great branches, which
spring in manner foresaid from the main
trunk of the tree, after diverging and separating
from each other, towards the east and west,
north, and south, come again together, and are
re-united with a crown, made of oak, olive,
myrtle, and laurel.

27

And the sun-beams of heaven, and the dews
thereof, and the spirits of departed patriots, cherish and nourish this tree, which is seemly to
behold, and fair to look upon.

28

Now, all the people of Albion rejoiced, and
were exceeding glad under the tree, as their

forefathers had been in the old times before them; and many persons in like manner came from afar, and from distant lands, to take shelter, and be happy under this blessed tree, and to partake of the goodly fruits thereof.

29

And a loud and warning voice spake, and said, " O people of Albion, beware, for whosoever shall apply the hatchet to the trunk, or mighty branches of this fair and beautiful tree, shall be deemed guilty of parricide."

30

" For the sap of the tree is of the blood of your fathers, which was shed in training and defending it, and which it imbibed in its growth."

31

" And from the bleeding wounds which the unhallowed hand may inflict upon the tree, there shall issue a pestilential and devouring flame, which shall desolate the land, and consume the people who dwell therein."

CHAP. VI.

1. How the people of Albion resisted the temptations of the idol.—2. Are hated by the Gauls, and the tyrant Napoleon, who plotteth their destruction, and sweareth vengeance against them, and their good king Albanus.

Now, it so happened, that amongst this happy and blessed people, there had been few worshippers of the first idol of the Gauls, that was called Licentiousness, and which was overthrown, as before written, by the power of Napoleon, the second idol; and it had pleased the Lord to convert the hearts of those few, and they repented them of their wickedness, and espied the danger and error of their evil ways, and rejoiced in their hearts, that the coming to pass of their foolish dreams, and vain imaginations, had been averted by the hand of God; therefore, it seemed good unto the Lord, not to deliver this people into the hands of their enemies.

2

For the king of the Albions, and his counsellors, perceived from the beginning the iniquity and deformity of the first idol, and they
warned the Albions, and all nations to beware
thereof; but the evil spirit, had, as before written, hardened the hearts, and darkened the understandings, of other nations, so they listened
not unto the voice of wisdom and of counsel.

3

But it had pleased the LORD to open the
hearts, and enlighten the understanding of the
people of Albion, and they resisted the temptations of the idol, feared the LORD, and honour-
ed the king.

4

Therefore the LORD blessed them in their
store, and in their outgoings and incomings;
and behold every man worshipped under his
own vine, and under his own fig-tree, and there
was no one to make him afraid.

5

And it came to pass, that the Gauls took of-
fence at this good king, and his chosen people,

because they mocked and despised the idol, and cleaved unto the only true God.

6

So they swore enmity against good king Albanus, the king of the Albions, and his people, and raged against them furiously, and threatened to overthrow them, and smite them from off the face of the earth.

7

And it moreover came to pass, that after the overthrow of the first idol, the second idol, which was the man Napoleon, threatened to do so in like manner, for he hated good king Albanus, and his people, with exceeding great hatred; because they had stood fast against him, and had foretold his cunning and deceit, and evil designs, unto the surrounding nations, who had fallen victims to the dominion of the idol, by reason of the deafness of their ears, and the iniquity and stubborness of their hearts.

8

Now, Napoleon grieved sore at the prosperity and happiness of good king Albanus, and his people; and amidst all his victories, and although surrounded with pomp, majesty, and power, nevertheless envy, wrath, and revenge, lurked and burned within him, even unto the exceeding great bitterness of his soul.

9

And it came to pass that his wrath and indignation could no longer be concealed, therefore it burst forth like unto a smothered flame; and he summoned his cunning and wise men, and the captains of his hosts together, and counselled with them, and plotted the overthrow and destruction of good king Albanus, and his happy, free, and faithful people.

10

And when the wise men, and the captains of the hosts of the Gauls, were assembled together, they prostrated themselves before the throne of the idol Napoleon, who spake unto them these words:

11

"Wise men and counsellors! by means of your wisdom and counsel, which reacheth from the earth beneath unto the heaven above, aided by my own unmeasurable genius and fortune, hath this mighty throne been raised, on which

you now behold me, seated in awful majesty
and power, encircled and surrounded by many
lesser thrones, principalities, and powers, of
my own creation, and all acknowledging and
paying homage and obeisance unto me."

12

" Brave captains of my numerous and invincible hosts, companions of my many and direful
battles, sharers of my victories, and my glory;
by means of your skill and courage in war, under my auspices, nation after nation, and
people after people, have been conquered and
overthrown; and many kings, princes, and po-
tentates, once great and glorious, but now humbled and fallen, have become tributary unto
me, and have been delivered into my hand."

13

" The measure of my happiness and ambition
would thus appear unto you to be full, but
there is yet one king, and one people, that
while he reigns, and they live, my rising
up, and my down laying, my outgoing, and
incoming, shall be unto me gall and bitterness."

14

So the wise men and counsellors, and the

captains of the hosts, lifted up their voices a-
loud and exclaimed, " Speak thy pleasure, *O
mighty Conqueror* "

15

So Napoleon yet again opened his mouth and
spake, and said unto them, " Yea verily, while
king Albanus reigns, and his people live, the
measure of my ambition shall not be filled,
nor the greatness and happiness of your king
completed, for unto the dominion over the land,
which has been given unto me, must be added
the dominion over the sea also."

16

" Go therefore, ye wise and cunning men,
and counsel together, and obtain for me *" ships,
commerce, and colonies,"* and cause forests to be
hewn down, and let artificers build ships and
vessels in my many harbours ; and go also in
like manner, ye captains of my mighty and
numerous hosts, and lead powerful armies to
the sea-coast, which is over against the land of
the Albions, and pass over to the land thereof, in the ships and vessels which shall be so
built."

17

" And having passed over the sea which divideth the land of Gaul from the land of Albion, slay the people thereof, with ignominious and bloody deaths, sack and burn their cities, towns, and villages, and pillage their houses, for my wrath against this people is exceeding great."

18

" And ye shall make the land desolate and barren like unto a wilderness, and I will reward you with the spoils and great riches thereof."

19

" And ye shall lead the sons and daughters of the Albions into captivity, and not a vestige shall be left of this once great, rich, and powerful people, save in the record of my mighty deeds."

20

And when the wise men, and counsellors, and the captains of the hosts of Napoleon, heard these things, they were sorely troubled and afflicted at heart; for they did not know in what manner they should pass over the sea, which divideth the land of Gaul from the land of Albion, because they had neither ships nor vessels wherein to pass over the sea, which was deep and mighty, and over which king Albanus already had the dominion.

21

But they durst not gainsay Napoleon, nevertheless they rose and went away, grieved and troubled in spirit, shouting with their lips, while their hearts were far from him, " O Emperor, live for ever!"

CHAP. VII.

1. *The Threats of the Gauls, and of the Tyrant, come to the ears of the Albions, who accordingly make mighty preparations to resist their foes.—2. The people of Albion cleave to their king and native land, and rise as one man to oppose the Tyrant and his hosts, who dread the sea and the valour of the Albions, by sea and land.*

AND when the tidings of these things, and the threatenings of the mighty conqueror, came to the ears of good king Albanus, he called together his counsellors and his nobles, and the great assembly of the nation, and the captains of his fleets and of his armies, to take counsel concerning the safety and defence of the land.

2

But lo and behold, when the people of Albion heard and saw the danger of their beloved king, and of the land of their fethers, and of the numberless and invaluable blessings which it had pleased God to bestow upon them, they rose of their own accord, as one man, and tendered unto the king their bodies and lives, without money and without price, to serve as a bulwark, and as a wall of defence around his throne, and the land over which he had ruled for many years in gentleness and mercy.

3

Now noble, and ignoble, rich and poor, young and old, yea almost all the males of the land of Albion, took up arms together and mingled in the ranks, and filled the hosts of king Albanus; until they became like unto the mighty and resistless river of the valley, which fed by many torrents from the mountains, after it hath rained, and the windows of heaven have been opened for many days, overfloweth its banks, and covereth the wide plain.

4

Now when good king Albanus saw his brave

and loving subjects of all ranks and conditions, rally around him in this manner, as never men had done before, his heart was moved with gladness, and he wept from the joy thereof.

5

But behold the tears which he shed were not tears of sorrow, for they were mixed with gratitude to God, for his exceeding goodness, and love to his people, for their exceeding affection.

6

In like manner the ships and fleets of good king Albanus, multiplied exceedingly in number, and the captains, sailors, and mariners thereof, were brave, and bold as lions.

7

Now, it came to pass, that numerous fleets and ships went forth, and great battles were fought on the face of the mighty waters, which wash the foundations of the round world; but, as before written, it had pleased the Lord to give unto good king Albanus, the dominion over the sea, and the brave captains of his ships, and his fleets, and the invincible sailors and mariners thereof, careless of the dangers of the deep, and of the terrible storms of heaven, mixed in direful conflict with the ships and fleets of the Gauls, and other nations, and either sunk them in the mighty waters, burned and destroyed them on the face thereof, or carried them in triumph into the harbours of the land of Albion.

8

And the power of good king Albanus continued to encrease on the mighty deep, and no ship dared to appear, or be seen, on the face thereof, save by his permission; and when the Gauls, and the other nations upon earth, saw and beheld the greatness of the deeds of the captains and sailors of good king Albanus, they marvelled one with another, and were sore afraid.

9

And when the captains and officers of the fleets and armies of the Albions fell in the midst of the battles and victories of their country, the king rewarded their wives, children, and kinsmen, with honour, wealth, and power, and monuments were raised in remembrance of their glorious deeds.

10

And, in like manner, when the sailors, soldiers, and mariners, fell in the same good cause, their wives, children, and kinsmen, were also taken care of, and cherished by their country, with exceeding great love and affection; so that every man rejoiced, and gloried to die in defence of his native land.

11

Now, when Napoleon beheld his ships and fleets taken and destroyed, as above written, and that the armies of king Albanus had multiplied like unto the sands of the sea, and covered the whole coast opposite to the land of Gaul, he was exceeding wroth, and swore and blasphemed, because he foresaw that the Lord would not deliver this king and his people into his hands, after the manner of other nations, who had been seduced by his crafts and subtleties, and had been accordingly punished for their great unrighteousness.

12

And, in like manner, when the captains and soldiers, of the hosts of the Gauls, saw that the sea which divideth the land of Gaul from

the land of Albion, was exceeding mighty
and deep, and that there were no ships wherein to pass over the same, and that the dominion over the sea was altogether in the hands of
king Albanus, their hearts failed them.

13

And moreover, when the Gauls saw that great
and powerful armies were drawn up on the coast
of Albion, ready to drive them and their tyrant
back again into the sea, and overwhelm them
therein, they abated and assuaged in their
pride and vain boasting, and sought to tarry on
the dry land, whereon they were encamped, and
had pitched their tents.

CHAP. VIII.

CHAP. VIII.

1. The ships of war which carried the army of the Gauls into Egypt are destroyed in a dreadful battle, by a Captain of the navy of King Albanus —2. The armies of the Albions thereafter defeat those of the Gauls wheresoever they meet.—3. The Albions rescue the land of Egypt from the Gauls.—4. The chief of the army of the Albions falls in battle.—5. The Gauls are afterwards defeated by the Albions in the land of Calabria.

AND it came to pass, that the fleet of king Albanus followed to the coast of Egypt, the ships of war which had carried the army of the Gauls, under Napoleon, to the land thereof.

2

Now, the Gauls had drawn up their ships in battle array, near unto the shore, therefore they bade defiance to the fleet of the Albions.

3

But the leader thereof was a brave and daunt- less man, and he fell upon the ships of the Gauls, and took and destroyed almost the

whole thereof, and killed the chief captain of
their fleet.

4

And when Napoleon, and his army, saw
these things, they were sorely troubled and dis-
mayed, and bade a long farewell to the land of
their fathers.

5

Nevertheless they went on as before written,
and conquered the land of Egypt, and threatened the holy city.

6

Soon thereafter, Napoleon having forsaken
his army in this distant land, suddenly returned to Gaul, having escaped the ships of the Albions, which were laying in wait to take him
prisoner; but it did not at this time please the
LORD to deliver him into the hands of the Albions.

7

And it came to pass, in like manner, that an
army of the Albions followed the army of the
Gauls into the land of Egypt.

8

And the Gauls came down to the sea coast

to oppose the Albions; but being unable to resist the valour of the hosts thereof, the Albions gained the dry land, and encamped thereon.

9

Soon thereafter a pitched battle was fought betwixt the two armies, in a plain near unto the city of Alexandria.

10

And it pleased the LORD to give unto the Albions the victory over their enemies, whom they overthrew with terrible slaughter.

11

But the Albions lost many men of valour, captains as well as soldiers, and the land of Pharaoh, and the inhabitants thereof, even unto this day, bear testimony to their glory.

12

Alas! there fell on that day, the chief leader of the army of the Albions, an aged warrior of great renown.

13

His hoary head was laid low on the plain, and his grey hairs mingled with the sands of Egypt.

14

Nevertheless, his spirit ascended on high on the wings of victory, and his fame flew abroad amongst the sons of men.

15

His precious remains were not buried in a strange land; but were restored by a loving army, to an admiring king and people.

16

While the Nile, the father of waters, continueth to flow, so long shall the fame of this aged warrior flourish in his native land, and in the land of Egypt, which he delivered from its enemies.

17

Again it came to pass, that another pitched battle was fought in the land of Calabria, betwixt the Albions and Gauls, and again it pleased the God of battles to give the victory unto the Albions.

18

For as the Albions were invincible, so in like manner were they incorruptible, and the gold and silver, and precious things wherewith the tyrant had corrupted the chiefs and soldiers of other nations, he dared not tender unto those of Albion, knowing well, that they would spurn them with disdain and indignation.

19

Now the renown of the armies of the Albions, and of their chiefs, spread abroad throughout the earth, and was a terror unto their enemies.

CHAP. IX.

1. The dominion of the Tyrant extendeth itself upon the face of the earth.—2. He continueth to deceive the Kings and Princes thereof, and the people over whom they reigned.—3. Some are overthrown by open force, others soothed and beguiled, until a convenient season arriveth for their complete and final destruction.

Now, the tyrant Napoleon continued to extend his dominion, and, as before written, nation after nation, and people after people, came one by one under the yoke of his power.

2

And he used soothings and blandishments

with one king or prince, until he directed the whole of his mighty force against another, and thereby overthrew him, and blotted him, and his people, from amongst the number of the nations, and kings of the earth.

3

But when a suitable season arrived, he broke faith with the king, or prince, to whom he had pretended friendship, and whom under false promises and assurances he had soothed and deceived.

4

And behold there was a queen, who had often paid unto the tyrant a ransom for the safety and preservation of herself and her kingdom : But this tyrant, not satisfied with ransom after ransom, aimed at the subjugation of this queen, and her kingdom.

5

And it so happened, that this queen possessed dominions in a far distant country, which is separated from the land in which she dwelt by great and mighty seas.

6

Foreseeing therefore, and being foretold, the

D

destruction which awaited her, and the land wherein she lived, she, and the prince her son, gathered together many ships, and much treasure, and all the nobles and people that were willing to seek shelter in this far distant country, and flee from the yoke of the tyrant, and the evil which was to come.

7

In like manner, good king Albanus, and his people, sent ships to assist this queen, and her prince, nobles, and people, in eschewing the evil wherewith they were threatened.

8

So they went into the ships that were thus prepared for them, and were wafted over the great ocean unto this far distant land, abounding in gold, and silver, and precious stones, wherein a new and mighty empire, beyond the reach of the tyrant, is now founded, under the dominion of this queen, and the prince her son.

9

And behold the sails of their vessels were scarcely spread to the winds of heaven, when the hosts of the tyrant were seen in many thousands, covering as a devouring flame the native land which the inhabitants thereof had been obliged to forsake for succour and for safety.

10

Nevertheless, they were beyond the reach of their enemies, being upon the sea, and under the protection of the invincible navy of king Albanus.

11

And the tyrant seized upon another, and still more powerful kingdom, which had for many years aided him and his designs, with its blood and its treasure, and he laid hold of its towns, and cities, and covered the land with his hosts.

12

And he stole the king thereof, his queen and the prince their son, and led them into captivity.

13

And he placed on the throne, on which this king and his forefathers had sat for many generations, a near kinsman, yea a brother of his own, who had no right or title thereto.

14

And the people of this oppressed kingdom, rose up against the deceitful tyrant, and demanded that their king, queen, and prince, and the freedom of the land should be restored unto them.

15

But the tyrant was inexorable, and he sent still greater and more powerful hosts against the people, and slew all those that were found in arms.

16

And he crowned his brother, and made him ruler over this people, while the streets of their cities were yet reeking with the blood of the brave defenders of their lawful king and native land.

17

Now good king Albanus, and his people, had sent fighting men and treasure, and all manner of warlike instruments to the assistance of this oppressed country; but the power and quickness of the tyrant, and his skill in war were exceeding great, and he overthrew the armies of the captive king, before those of the Albions could come up to their aid.

18

And lo! when the tyrant beheld an army of good king Albanus on his own side of the sea, he rejoiced in his heart, and profanely said; " Now it hath pleased the Lord to give me vengeance against this king, and his people, for I shall put their hosts to the sword, and not a man amongst them shall return to his native land, to tell the direful tidings."

19

" In the land of Albion I shall cause streams of tears to flow."

20

" Her mothers shall bewail their youthful and warlike sons slain by Gallic swords."

21

" Her helpless orphans shall lisp and weep the fall of many a fond father."

22.

So he hastened together, · by long and tiresome marches, his desperate and blood-thirsty legions, and flew from the capital of his mighty

D 3

empire, and put himself at the head of his armies.

23

But behold the hosts of the Albions had, ere this, landed on the tyrant's side of the sea, and had overthrow none of his armies with great slaughter, and had caused them to quit the country of the exiled queen, wherein they then were, and whereupon they had unlawfully seized in manner above written.

24

And in this battle the skill of the chiefs and captains, and the valour of the soldiers of king Albanus shone exceedingly; yea truly to their own immortal glory, and the terror and dismay of their enemies.

25

Now it so happened, that the tyrant continued to wax exceeding wroth, and again swore, that not a man of this army of the Albions should ever return to his native land.

26

Nevertheless, he advanced not against them himself; but sent one of the captains of his hosts, with a numerous army, to drive the Albions into the sea, while he looked on afar off.

27

But the brave captain who led the army of good king Albanus first into the country, to succour the inhabitants thereof, and thereafter back unto the coast, through dangers and difficulties, greater than ever army had met before, bade defiance to the hosts of the Gauls, and when he came to the sea-side, he gave them battle, and covered the plain with their dead.

28

They retreated, terrified and appalled, nor did they seek further to [molest the Albions, whom they permitted to go into the ships which were prepared to receive them.

29

But, alas! in this glorious, but direful battle, there fell many valiant men, and in the midst of them, covered with glory, and crowned with victory, their brave and skilful chief, whose name now stands high in the temple of Fame.

30

And the king of the Albions, and all his people mourned exceedingly over the fall of this great man.

31

´ Nay, the very enemy which he had conquered, gave testimony of the admiration and reverence in which they held the warlike virtues of this departed hero.

32

Nevertheless, it pleased the Lord to deliver for a time, this devoted land, and the dwellers therein, into the hands of the tyrant, who conquered the same, and kept the king, queen, and prince thereof, in dreary and sorrowful captivity.

33

But a voice coming as it were from heaven, spake and said, " O people of Iberia, be of good courage, and persevere in your noble and patriotic exertions in behalf of your king and native land, under the happy assurance, that by the blessing of Providence, they shall be crowned with ultimate and glorious success."

CHAP. X.

CHAP. X.

1. Wise Counsellors, and mighty Captains of hosts and of ships, with whom it pleased the Lord to bless King Albanus.—2. He is deprived of some of them by death. —3. Lamentations for the loss thereof.

Now, as before written, it had pleased the Lord in these latter and troublesome times, to bless good king Albanus, with great statesmen, and counsellors, excelling in wisdom, and in speech.

2

And behold, the king and his people looked up to those men for succour and for safety, under the blessing of Providence, against the mischievous machinations of the cunning tyrant, and the dangers wherewith the nation was environed.

3

But behold it pleased the Lord to remove from this lower world, several of those great and excellent statesmen.

4

Their earthly remains were, amidst the lamentations of sorrowing, and admiring friends, deposited in the silent, and almost mutual grave.

5

The memory of their excellences shall nevertheless live for ever in the bosom of posterity!

6

Their glorious spirits shall shine as bright stars in the firmament of fame!

7

And behold it is the prayer of the king and his people, that succeeding counsellors may be inspired with the same patriotism and wisdom, which distinguished those sage men now no more.

8

That the radiant and resplendent brilliancy of their great souls, may serve as a light or beacon, to direct the counsels and actions of those, who now, or in time coming, may be placed at the helm of the state.

9

And the king and all the people prayed, that the guardian and angel spirit of pure and unpolluted patriotism, might direct the counsels of the land of Albion, during the perils and troubles wherewith it was beset on ever side.

10

As before written, it had in like manner pleased the LORD, to deprive this king and his people, of mighty and renowned chiefs and captains of hosts and fleets, who fell in the midst of glory and of victory.

11

And amongst the captains of the fleets of the Albions, there was a man, whose name was known in the remotest corner of the earth, and who was an exceeding terror unto all the enemies of his country.

12

Now this man pursued even unto utter destruction all the ships on the face of the ocean, that bade defiance unto those of king Albanus.

13

His fame waxed exceeding great, and all the ends of the earth bore witness unto it.

14

By the blessing of God he broke in twain, with terrible overthrow, the leagues and combinations that were plotting by the tyrant, and his satellites, against king Albanus and his

people, and drove them like chaff before the
wind.

15

They vanished at his presence, as does the
morning vapour before the bright beams of the
sun; or like the dark cloud, when it is burst
asunder, and scattered by the lightning and
the tempest.

16

Now it came to pass, that the ships of the
Gauls, and of their allies, gathered together,
yet once more, and tempted to battle the fleets
of good king Albanus, which were commanded
by this mighty man of war.

17

And when they were thus gathered together,
he fell upon them, and overthrew them, with
terrible destruction; and lo! hardly a single
ship escaped from his fury.

18

And he gave the carcases of the enemies of
his country unto the fowls of heaven, and the
fishes of the sea.

19

For lo and behold, the face of the mighty

deep was covered with thousands of their slain.

20

But, alas! in the midst of this direful conflict, the great captain of the fleet of the Albions fell!

21

His departing spirit flew on high, on the golden wings of victory, and took up its abode in the mansions of immortal glory!

22

And lo! as the hero fell, the ocean heaved a sigh of lamentation, for she had rejoiced to bear on her mighty billows a warrior of such great renown, and who had for many years been the companion of her wondrous ways.

23

She had witnessed the calmness of his soul, amidst the ragings of the hideous storms and tempests which trouble her great waters.

24

She had moreover admired his exceeding skill and valour, in the terrible battles which he had fought and conquered, in the various climes to which she had borne him in proud triumph,

to the confusion and dismay of the enemies of
his country.

25

So also the hearts of those valiant sailors and
mariners, which no tempest had ever appalled,
and which no foe had ever daunted, melted into sorrow.

26

For lo ! the sailors and mariners of Albion,
wept over the fall of their adored chief, now no
more !

27

Behold the banners of many nations, conquered on the deep, shroud the proud tomb of
the hero !

28

And king Albanus, and all his people, in
like manner, lamented the fall of this matchless
man.

29

His resplendent spirit shines as a polar star
in the bright firmament of fame !

30

It is in the midst of a group of departed heroes, and many there be amongst the warriors

of the Albions, now on earth, who press eager-
ly to join this glorious constellation by aiming
at the palm of victory and renown.

31

And behold, when the tidings of the death of
these great counsellors and warriors of the Albions, reached the ears of Napoleon, who hated
and feared them in his heart, he grinned a
smile of devilish gladness.

32

Such as is to be seen on the meagre visage of
the spectre of death, when his hungry eye sur-
veys a field of battle, heaped with innumerable
slain.

33

Or such a smile, as Satan, the enemy of
mankind, is supposed to grin, when good and
holy men are removed from this lower world;
whose pious example, and virtuous struggles,
had saved thousands of their fellow-creatures,
from his hellish grasp.

CHAP. XI.

1. The Oak of Albion.—2. He claimeth the sovereignty
of the Wood and of the Flood.

Now the oak, when he reared his proud head
in the forests of Albion, thus spake unto the
other trees thereof:

2

" Behold, arising in the midst of you, the
monarch of the wood, and of the flood also !"

3

" When this adamantine trunk, and these
brawny arms of mine; shall have outlived an
hundred years, and ten thousand storms, I shall
only fall to rise more glorious !"

4

" Then shall I become as a mighty castle on
the deep, riding triumphant on the billow and
in the storm !"

5

" In my stupendous bosom shall be contained an host of heroes, hardy and invincible as

myself, proof against the storm and the tempest."

6

" From my dark irony sides the dauntless sons
of Albion shall dart the lightning, and hurl the
thunder-bolt."

7

" The oak of other lands, when it shall come
into contact with me, and the warriors within
me, shall be as the cyprus ; a coffin, in which
the enemy of Albion shall either find a burn-
ing, or a watery grave."

8

" Around the isle of Albion I shall ride as a
guardian and protecting angel ; but unto distant and hostile lands I shall carry terror and
dismay."

9

" When I shall glide in proud majesty along
the sea-girt side of my native mountain or valley, let the oak of Albion behold from afar her
kindred king, and hasten to be like unto him in
majesty and power, and let all the trees of the
forest in submission wave their humbler heads."

10

Now when the oak of Albion had ceased speaking, all the trees of the forest gave a nod of obeisance unto him ; nay, the oaks of other lands did so in like manner.

11

Yea all the people of the earth were compelled to proclaim the oak of Albion the chiefest among trees, the monarch of the wood, and of the tide also.

12

And those who fought within his wooden walls, and in his floating citadel, were proclaimed in like manner by all the earth, with one assent, to be the boldest and bravest, nay, the very chiefest of heroes.

CHAP. XII.

CHAP. XII.

I. The Kings and Princes of the earth are warned of the crafts and subtleties of the Tyrant.—2. Virtue is recommended as the only secure foundation of the kingdoms of this earth.—3. The solidity of the Empire of Almighty God ascribed amongst other things to the sense felt by created existence of the purity and holiness of the Great Governor of all things.

EMPERORS, kings, and princes, and all ye dwellers upon earth, beware of the crafts and subtleties of this hellish tyrant.

2

For he intwineth himself like a serpent around those he meaneth to destroy, and whispereth soft, blandishing, and deceitful things in their ears, until a convenient season arriveth for stinging them to death.

3

He holds out a phial of oil and honey, with which he smoothes his way ; but when the

hour of his action cometh, the cloven foot shew-
eth itself, and forthwith are poured gall and
wormwood, into those who had drunk of his
sweet, but deceitful cup.

4

His open force and warfare are not so much
to be dreaded, as his secret machinations, and
pretended friendships; nor is the armour of the
tyrant more terrible than his traiterous shield,
and purple mantle.

5

Emperors, kings, princes, and people, fear
the only true and living God, and keep his
commandments and precepts, as revealed unto
you in holy writ.

6

Be assured, that no earthly throne can be
secure, and that no people can be safe or happy, unless religion and morality be the foundation and ground work thereof.

7

Behold, as the man who giveth himself up to
unrighteousness is despised of men, and cometh
to utter ruin and destruction, so in like manner
doth the prince and his people.

8

If, therefore, the prince of a land be not religious and virtuous, in the practice of his life,
and if his people be not so in like manner, but
on the contrary; then be assured, the hour of
their common destruction is most certainly at
hand, and the Lord will either deliver them
into the hands of their enemies, or afflict them
with direful evils, such as civil war, pestilence,
and famine.

9

Take example of these truths, O kings,
princes, and people, from the events which have
passed before you in your own days.

10

For year after year, nay, day after day, kings
have been overthrown, and nations destroyed,
because they were full of rottenness and corruption, and had sunk into all manner of depravity and wickedness.

11

It behoveth those, therefore, who expect to
escape the general destruction that prevaileth,
and the vengeance of a just and angry God, to
consider what manner of men they are, and to

amend their ways, so that they may in time coming, live a godly, religious, and sober life.

12

All men must confess, because they have seen it with their eyes, and heard it with their ears, and in their own times, that no rank, power, or wealth, however great and exalted, can supply the want of genuine virtue and morality, or save from that ruin and contempt which fall on the heads of worthless and wicked men.

13

Vice and licentiousness overthrow the prince as well as the peasant, for the laws of a pure and just God know no distinction of persons.

14

Now, in proof of these doctrines, hath it not so happened amongst the recent destruction of numerous kings and princes, the desolation of their empires, and punishment of their people, that the king who ruleth over the Albions is almost the only one, among the other rulers of the earth, who has preserved his throne, and the love, affection, and admiration of his people?

15

Say, therefore, whether the preservation of this king's throne, the love, affection, and admiration of his people, have not been the just reward of his piety and devotion, and of the many virtues which adorn his character, all which are highly pleasing in the sight of God?

16

Now, if the conception be not too great and daring for man, may not an example of this truth be drawn from the great Creator and Governor of all things, the King of kings, and Lord of lords?

17

May not the eternal solidity of the inconceivable empire of Almighty God, and the unchangeable harmony and obedience which pervade all his wondrous works, derive as much strength from the universal adoration in which his unerring truth, his immaculate purity and holiness, and his inflexible justice are held, by created existence, as from the immensity and grandeur of his unmeasurable power?

18

Behold all the rivers of the earth glide with

one assent unto the sea, and the sea herself eb-
beth and floweth at her stated periods and appointed seasons !

19

The thunders roll, and the hills re-echo the
terrible voice thereof!

20

The storm rageth on the face of the great
waters, and in the darkness of the night !

21

The mountains are shaken from their foundations, and laid low; and the vallies are raised
up in their stead!

22

The sun, moon, and stars, perform their glorious and appointed revolutions, and all the
works of creation proceed in beauteous and regular order!

23

Ye rivers, why do ye glide into the ocean,
sea, why dost thou ebb, and flow, and raise thy
mighty billows to the skies ?

24

Ye mountains, why do ye tremble and sink
low, ye vallies why are ye exalted ?

25

Ye thunders, why do ye roll; how cometh it, ye storms, that ye rage on the mighty deep, and in the darkness of the night?

26

Whence are thy glories, O sun, moon, and stars, and whence thy wondrous revolutions?

27

And behold the sea and all the great works of nature rejoined, " In these things we feel and obey the conscious voice of a great and holy Creator, at whose word we tremble!"

28

" It is God, yea even our own God, that worketh all these marvellous deeds!"

29

Learn then, O man, that virtue and religion are the only true and solid pillars of the feeble fabrics erected by thee in this lower world.

30

That truth, holiness, and justice, are the peculiar attributes of thy God, and give immutable and eternal duration to all his great and wondrous works, which loudly proclaim a consciousness thereof.

CHAP. XIII.

1. The People of Albion are told of their increasing wickedness and licentiousness, and are admonished accordingly.—2. Their manners are inveighed against, and they are summoned to repentance and amendment of life.

Now it came to pass, that the first idol, namely Licentiousness, whereof mention is made in the beginning of this Book, began in these latter times to gain many worshippers and followers in the land of Albion.

2

Various kinds of wickedness, such as adultery, uncleanness, drunkenness, and the like, made progress in the land, and pervaded all ranks and conditions of people.

3

Many of the great and the rich, spent their time in nightly revels, and lived in the open contempt and neglect of the holy ordinances of religion.

4

Therefore they were hated and despised, by those of inferior station, who looked forward with eagerness to the time of their final over-throw and destruction.

5

Those of mean station, on the other hand, gave themselves up to drunkenness, and lying, the fruits whereof, are poverty and wretched ness, disease, theft, murder, and divers other crimes and evils.

6

By the great and the rich, day was turned into night, and night into day, and in this man-ner sober-mindedness was perverted and done away, and the regular ordinations of the Gover-nor of the universe outraged.

7

The sun, who came forth in the morning like a bridegroom from his eastern chamber, arrayed in all his dazzling glories, to cheer and enlighten a benighted world, to dissipate the dreary darkness of the night, and awaken drow-sy nature to joy and gladness; found this gene-ration of bats and of owls, male and female,

revelling in all manner of riot and licentiousness.

8

The returning day chased them away, and
compelled them to seek their lurking places,
weary and worn out with their nightly and dis-
orderly vigils.

9

There again they wallow in listless, and de-
praved effeminacy and luxury, until the glorious luminary of day has nearly gone down to
his western chamber; leaving the pale moon,
the companion of the silence of the night, to
witness those things, which had shunned the
test of the broad and brilliant day.

10

How comes it then, O man, that thou pre-
ferrest the night to the day? Is it because thy
deeds are evil?

11

But doth it not occur to thy mind, that be-
sides depraving thy soul by doing so, thou moreover outragest and profanest the beauteous and
regular ordinations of thy Creator, who has or-
dained the sun to rule by day, and the moon

to rule by night, and has given unto all things their appointed seasons?

12

Say are thy days too long upon the land, that the sun is thus irksome unto thee, and that thou art desirous to foretaste the dreary night of death?

13

What, O man, O guilty man, who thus insultest the orderly appointments of heaven, what would not thy consternation be, were the sun to loiter on his eastern couch, and the return of morning to be withheld but for a little while beyond its appointed time, and thus to leave the world to utter darkness and dismay?

14

Now, out of these nightly revels spring adultery, and many other deadly sins.

15

And the good and wise men of Albion beheld these evils spreading with fear and trembling, because they had been the forerunners of the destruction of the nations which had fallen around them in their own days.

16

O adultery, thy wages on earth ought to be an ignominious death !

17

Thou art indeed a deadly poison, a genuine murderer!

18

Father, mother, children, friend ; nay, often whole nations cruelly perish through thy hellish influence!

19

Stop then, O people of Albion, ere it be too late, the tide of your increasing wickedness, so as to avert the evils which have befallen other nations, and the vengeance that must infallibly overtake you in like manner, unless you accept of warning in due time

20

Learn to appreciate and preserve the blessings which it hath pleased God in his infinite goodness to bestow upon you.

21

Unto you have been given a pure religion, wholesome laws, a good and pious king.

22

The land in which you have been appointed to dwell, is girded round with a guardian ocean, over which you have obtained the dominion.

23

By means thereof, there is wafted to your shores, in innumerable ships, the produce of all the nations of the earth.

24

The sea which washeth your winding shores teems with fish, fit for the food and nourishment of man.

25

Your mountains are covered with sheep and cattle, and your vallies with rich crops of corn.

26

Peace and plenty reign in the land, and the people thereof ought to be exceeding glad.

27

For behold, the God of armies has turned the attle far from your gates; and although the direful contest may prevail in distant lands, yet the fields of Albion are free from the stain either of kindred or foreign blood, nor does the storm of war rage throughout the land.

28

Peaceful are her cities, towns, and villages, her cottages, and her shadowy and rural places.

29

Nor is the sound of the murderous cannon to be heard, nor the glittering of arms to be seen in any part of the land; save when the good tidings of victories gained in far countries, or on the mighty deep, are proclaimed, the natal day of good king Albanus commemorated, or the like.

30

For the battles of Albion are fought on the face of the mighty deep, and the din thereof is either drowned in the roaring billow and in the storm, or dies away on the smooth face of the watery waste, far from the ear of the husbandman.

31

The streets of her cities do not reek with blood, nor are her green pastures stained with gore.

32

The blood of her enemies floweth and is dissolved in the briny deep, which openeth itself to

receive their carcases, and deliver them for pas-
time to the ravenous fishes of the sea.

33

They are buried without the help of spade or
of shovel, and no pestilential breath can issue
from their graves.

34

Far different the people of other lands, whose
cities, towns, and villages, are burnt and destroyed, and whose cottages and fertile fields are laid
waste amidst the ravages of devouring armies.

35

Whose rivers are choked, and whose plains
are heaped with the unburied slain, from whose
putrifying corpses issue ten thousand diseases,
and as many deaths.

36

If, O people of Albion, ye are truly desirous
of preserving and enjoying the many and invaluable blessings which the goodness of Provi-
ence has vouchsafed to you, be thankful unto
God the giver.

37

Be ye righteous and hold fast your integrity,
therwise, as before written, ruin and desolation

must infalliably come upon the land, and the inhabitants thereof.

CHAP. XIV.

1. A mighty storm ariseth.—2. The vessel of the State is in danger of perishing.—3. A wise and good Counsellor pilots the vessel, and weathers the storm.—4. The vessel is brought into a safe harbour; but the pilot thereof dieth, through his endeavours to save the vessel.

Now, the passions of men, when they burst the bonds of true religion, and of the ancient and venerable laws of their fathers, may be likened unto the tempest, and whirlwind, the hail and the storm, when it pleaseth the Ruler thereof to let them loose from their abodes.

2

So in these latter days, religion being despised of men, and the laws of their fathers being in like manner contemned, tumult prevailed throughout the earth, and great was the devastation thereof.

3

Behold the clouds gather together, and become as utter darkness, the winds blow, and the sea is moved from her bed!

4

The vessels of many states are set adrift, and lose themselves in this tempestuous ocean.

5

And lo! for a season the vessel of the state of Albion, the favoured of Heaven, is driven from her anchor into this sea of troubles!

6

Now the safe haven is seen no more, and the firm land disappears!

7

The storm of anarchy rages throughout the earth, and blows with mighty fury.

8

Dreadful is the conflict, and terrible the uproar of human passions run mad!

9

Now the angry and impetuous billow raises the vessel to the skies, now it precipitates her into the watery valley.

11

Now she is hid in clouds and darkness,

her timbers crack, and her sails shiver in the storm !

12

And the king and people, and all that are in the vessel, cry aloud, " we shall surely perish."

13

Lo! the vessel is no longer to be seen, save when the lightning's gleam shews her in peril, and depicts the dreary abyss, wherein she is tossed to and fro.

14

Behold! that short-lived vivid torch of heaven; it shows a pilot at the helm !

15

Lo! his eagle eye is fixed on the polar star of ancient and venerable truth, for which he firmly steers !.

16

Now, he casts a smile of contumely on the scorn of men, and bids the tempest of their passions hush !

17

The spirits of the ancients of the land behold, from above, with anxious eye, the danger of the vessel wherein they had been happily wafted through their mortal state.

18

So they whispered to the pilot, amidst the jarring of the elements, and the crashing of empires; " Courage, and be of good cheer, O pilot, for thou shalt weather the storm, and bring the vessel committed to thy charge into a safe haven !"

19

Now the storm lasted for many days, and many ships with the people therein perished; but under the blessing of God, the vessel of the state of Albion was by her sage pilot, brought to anchor in a secure harbour.

20

But, alas! the many watchful and anxious nights which this pilot had spent, proved fatal unto him; and the storm had hardly ceased, and the calm returned, when in the midst of pious ejaculations for his country's good, he resigned his soul to him who gave it.

21

Now, if his departure from this world was mourned by the king and people, whom, by the grace of God, he had saved from peril and ruin, his arrival in the mansions of peace was greeted by the patriot and kindred spirits of the ancients of Albion.

22

And when the king and people, and all that were in the vessel, looked back, and thought upon the storm which they had escaped, they were sore afraid, and thanked God that he had delivered them in safety.

23

And a warning voice was heard amongst the people of Albion, saying, " O people, now that your enviable vessel is safely moored in harbour, beware of again driving her into open sea, by kindling the fury of your lawless passions, or the tempestuous ragings thereof; lest ye have not another pilot to weather the storm, and lest ye be doomed finally to perish therein."

CHAP. XV.

CHAP. XV.

LET each man amongst you try, and examine diligently his own heart, and thereupon repent, and amend his life, for by so doing, the general corruption of the land will be removed in the best, and most effectual manner.

2

For it is the wickedness and corruption of each man, which compose the aggregate wickedness and corruption of the commonwealth.

3

As it is not every one, say the holy scriptures, who crieth Lord, Lord! that shall enter into the kingdom of heaven; neither is it every one who crieth thief, thief! of his neighbour, that ought to enter into the kingdom of this world, or the management of the affairs thereof.

4

For who amongst you that revileth and up-braideth his neighbour, can say; " thank God, I am not like unto this man, a sinner ; neither do I err in thought, word, or deed."

5

Ye who descry the mote in your brother's eye, see, that there be not a beam in your own.

6

Lay your hands upon your hearts, and en-quire, on soul and conscience, whether ye have kept all the commandments of the Lord more scrupulously than your neighbour, and whether ye be in reality more pure and holy than those whom you accuse ?

7

For it is to be apprehended, that there are at all times amongst the raisers up of strife and contention, men of ruined and desperate means.

8

Men, who through their own licentiousness, prodigality, and extravagant living, have not left wherewithal to eat, and drink, and be clothed.

9

But who hope to gather a plentiful harvest, amidst the ruin and desolation of their country, and the wreck of their neighbour's estate.

10

Take heed, therefore, O people, that there be not amongst your clamorous and professed friends, " wolves in sheep's clothing !"

11

Napoleon, the tyrant, deceitful in heart, soft, yet inflammatory in speech, professeth himself, in like manner, to be a friend to the people, whom he stirreth up against their lawful governors, and deceiveth with vain promises and hopes; saying, that he will remove their burdens, and ameliorate their condition.

12

Yet doth not this very man, in whom the truth is not, cheat, rob, and murder the people every where, and involve them in universal thraldom, misery, and ruin ; and are not these things made manifest before your eyes ?

13

If it hath pleased God, O people of Albion, to afflict you with men resembling Napoleon in ambition, restlessness, deceit, and the holding out of promises which they know in their hearts to be false and vain ; God be praised that he hath not given unto them the power, nor girded them with the conquering sword of the cruel and blood-thirsty tyrant !

14

Be not misled, O people of Albion, by the heated and designing speeches of men, who associate with publicans and sinners, and meet for luxurious feastings, and immoderate revellings.

15

They seek to prey upon the vitals of the people, and nevertheless " mock the meat they feed on."

16

Beware, in like manner, of the glowing words, and cunning conceits, of modern and stripling philosophers, who have acquired a little bookish lore, and dangerous learning.

17

Rather incline your ears and your hearts to ancient truth, and pay respect to the hoary head, and wary hand of age.

18

Moreover, it is to be apprehended, that there are amongst the professed friends of liberty and equality, men of tyrannical and overbearing dispositions, devoted to change, restlessness, and ambition, irreligious in their doctrines, and licentious in their lives.

19

Men, ay churchmen too, cruel and tyrannical in their families, overbearing and supercilious towards their brethren of mankind; participators in political intrigues, animosities, and cabals; and associators with persons of libertine and licentious principles and practice.

20

Behold! how unlike such men are to the meek and lowly master, whose servants and followers they impiously and hypocritically profess themselves to be.

21

Place therefore, O people of Albion, your trust in God, and in your good old king and his counsellors, for the time being.

22

For by so doing, ye shall be rescued from

the dangers wherewith ye are threatened by evil and designing men; who, Napoleon like, seek to make you the tools of their own ambition and aggrandisement, and will, like him, deride and laugh you to scorn, and trample you under their feet, whensoever their own purposes are accomplished.

23

Finally, stand fast, O Albions, in the liberty wherewith God hath made you free, and be not again entangled in the snares of wicked and designing men, who from ambition, or for the sake of gain, seek violent and dangerous changes.

CHAP. XVI.

1. *The parable of the Bear and the Monkey.—2. The Monkey is suddenly changed into a Tyger, which devoureth the Bear, and scattereth his flesh and his bones to the winds of heaven.*

Now a riddle is put forth, and a parable is spoken, unto the people of the earth.

2

A great bear with brawny paws, and covered with long bristles, is brought forth in the north.

3

He stretcheth himself over many lands, and aweth much people, over whom the hail and the snow continually do pass.

4

Frozen seas and rivers, and plains covered with eternal frost, are unto him as dwelling places; and the storm which chilleth other beasts, even unto death, beateth upon him as upon a rock, which is covered with furs and with skins.

5

His nightly path is lighted by fiery spectres, that sport and dance along the polar sky, and play amidst the wintry stars.

6

Fierce is the bear, and not to be conquered by fear or force.

7

Now in the western regions there liveth an animal which is fashioned somewhat after the image of man, and is endowed with cunning, fawning, and deceit, and lo! this animal is called a monke .

8

Now the bear and the monkey having met each other, the bear was pleased with the monkey, who caressed and soothed him, and told him, what a mighty beast he was.

9

So the bear allowed the monkey from time to time to play and frisk around him ; but it came to pass, that the monkey having scratched the bear, he thereupon raised his bristles, and threatened to hug the monkey to death.

10

Nevertheless the monkey contrived yet again to soothe the bear, and he fawned upon him and caressed him, and whispered soft and pleasing things in his ear.

11

And the bear and the monkey became exceeding great friends, and met and communed together, and finally agreed to divide the north and the west betwixt them.

12

So they went on paw in paw, and the bear grinned smiles to the monkey, while the monkey played in sportive mirth around the bear.

13

Now it so happened, that the bear was lulled asleep by the soft fawnings of the monkey.

14

And in his sleep he dreamed a dream, and behold the dream was, that the monkey had put out one of his eyes, and bit in twain the strongest sinew in his most powerful paw.

15

So he awoke with a mighty growl, and rose in his wrath to destroy the monkey.

16

But lo! when he awoke from his dream, half blind, and half lame, he beheld before him no longer the feeble fawning monkey, his former friend and favourite; but a fierce and furious tyger, who at one dart devoured him, and seized as his prey the lands over which he had been in use to rule.

17

And the tyger tore the bear into pieces, and scattered his flesh and his bones to the winds of heaven.

18

For unto this monkey, in which there was

heretofore the heart, there has moreover been superadded the power and strength of the tyger.

CHAP. XVII.

The Vision of Eliakim.

Now it came to pass in the dread hour of night, when mortal man, and all living creatures, lay overwhelmed in sleep, that a vision appeared unto me.

2

Then I beheld, and lo! the likeness of an angel of heaven, clothed in a fine linen robe, white as snow, came unto me, and put forth the form of an hand !

3

And the angel lifted me up between the earth and the heavens, and carried me to the region of visions, and put me on an high place, that looketh towards the four corners of the earth !

4

Then he touched my sight, and said unto me, open thine eyes ; so I opened mine eyes, and beheld spread before me sundry lands, people, and languages.

5

And upon a throne, made of gold, and covered with crimson, raised as it were in the midst of the nations, I saw a man seated in great majesty and power.

6

And around the throne there stood multitudes of armed men, and captains of hosts, administering unto the will and pleasure of the man who was seated on the throne.

7

Now, while I was yet looking, he descended therefrom, and mounted a beast, like unto a dragon in shape and in kind, and the man and the dragon became as one ; and from the eyes thereof there proceeded flashes of devouring fire.

8

Then the angel said unto me, turn thine eyes the way toward the north; so I turned mine eyes the way toward the north.

But my vision being imperfect, I looked up to the firmament of heaven, to discover whence this gloomy light proceeded, and what might be the cause thereof.

And behold the sun which was in the firmament shone as it were through blood, and all things on earth reddened unto the eye.

Nevertheless, I could see the fiery dragon move with exceeding great quickness to and fro; and wheresoever he went, he was followed by the numerous captains of hosts, and the multitudes of armies, which I had observed standing and administering around the throne.

Now I saw these armies deal death, and spread desolation over the face of the earth.

And when the armies of other nations encountered those of the dragon, I beheld the plains of the earth beneath me heaped with slain, and the great rivers thereof, rolling purple streams and mangled corpses into the ocean.

14

Flames issued from the towns and cities of the land, and the lamentations of widows and orphans rent the skies !

15

Deep groans were heaved by the wounded and the dying ; and I saw as it were in the silent hour of night, ghosts stalking over the field of death !

16

See ! the thin and meagre spectre of famine crawls along the desolated plain !

17

Behold ! the sable image of pestilence comes to complete the unfinished work of the slaughtering sword, and chokes up the half filled sepulchre !

18

Now exceeding great fear and trembling seized my frame, and withdrawing mine eyes from this terrible sight, I turned them towards the angel for safety and consolation.

19

Nay, in the height of my terror, I endea-
voured to seize his hand; but the form thereof
eluded the touch of mortal man !

20

Nevertheless, I saw the angel turn aside and
weep, and behold a crystal drop fell upon the
skirts of his snow white raiment !

CHAP. XVIII.

The Vision Continued.

AND the angel said furthermore unto me,
turn thee yet again, and thou shalt see strange
things.

2

So my spirit revived within me, and I turned
yet again, and behold I saw mighty forges, and
from the forges there issued the sound of many
hammers; and I moreover heard the clanking
of chains, and saw many thousands of captives loaded therewith, coming and going different ways.

3

And the angel observing that I marvelled within myself, said unto me, behold the dragon who is at the head of the devouring armies thou seest, causeth the nations over which he ruleth to forge fetters for themselves.

4

And the thousands thou observest proceeding from the throne, goaded with chains, and guarded by soldiers, are the young men of the land, who, torn from their homes, their families, and friends, are forced to fill up the waste occasioned in the armies of the dragon by the sword which is without, and the pestilence and famine which rage within.

5

The thousands, again, whom thou seest returning from the armies without, and proceeding as it were towards the throne, covered with wounds, and loaded with chains, hungry, naked, and emaciated, are the captives which the dragon and his armies have taken in war; and those men in armour thou seest conducting them are the very same who, a short while before, were themselves dragged to the field of battle.

6

Moreover, sayeth the angel, not only do the nations thou beholdest work out the chains wherewith they are themselves fettered; but they moreover shed their blood in order to purchase them, as if bondage were as sweet, and as much to be prized as thou, " O thrice precious liberty !"

7

Then he said unto me, now behold the lesser thrones which surround the greater one, from which thou sawest the dragon descend, to spread on every side ruin and desolation, rapine, murder, and slavery.

8

So I turned mine eyes towards the thrones, and behold I saw them, in like manner as that of the dragon, by whom they had been reared, encircled and supported by blood-thirsty legions.

9

And the angel yet again desired me to turn mine eyes the way toward the north, and be-

hold I there saw a throne, on which was seated
a powerful ruler.

10

And around this throne there sat fawning
and deceitful men, who never ceased whispering in the ear of the man on the throne, soft
and blandishing things.

11

And this man having descended from the
throne, in the midst of his courtiers and flatter-
ers, went into his palace.

12

And the angel brought me, as it were, to the
gate of the palace; and when I looked, behold,
I saw women in loose and gay attire, and of
wanton looks and gestures, waiting the arrival
of the king.

13

And they also whispered soft and blandishing things in his ear, and gave strength to the
guile and deceit which the courtiers and flatter-
ers had been practising around the throne.

14

Now, the angel having again observed me to
marvel at these things, said, behold the flatter-

ers and courtiers whom thou sawest around the throne, and the cunning and deceitful women whom thou now seest in the palace, are hired by the dragon to divert the attention of the powerful monarch thou beholdest, from the designs of the dragon, that he may not be molested in the execution thereof, until a convenient season shall arrive for overthrowing the ruler of this nation also.

15

Now the angel bade me turn mine eyes once more towards the frightful and hideous prospect which lay spread before me.

16

Lo ! the heavenly and cheering voice of freedom was stilled, and not to be heard amongst the nations, and dreary and universal slavery seemed to prevail throughout the earth !

17

The tongue of the patriot orator was dumb, and sealed up ; the pen of the writer was taken from him !

18

The prison doors were ever grating on their

massy hinges, and the dreary dungeon was ever opening its hideous jaws!

19

And the angel of heaven brought me to the door of one of the many strong places which I beheld.

20

When lo! I saw in a horrid cell, a pale and emaciated prisoner, goaded with iron chains, pining away in dreary and forlorn confinement!

21

Hunger and disease were pourtrayed on his woe-worn countenance!

22

A tyrant's fiat had excluded him from the sweet society of men, and from the cheering light of the sun, and had doomed him to become a prey to corruption, and the reptiles of the earth!

23

Now when I beheld these things, my spirit failed me, and I would have sunk in grief and despair, had not the angel supported me.

24

And turning unto the angel, I said, How cometh it that the Lord doth not deliver the dragon into the hands of the people, that they may slay him, and thereby remove the direful sufferings of the nations ?

25

But behold the angel looked me in the face and chid me, saying; Knowest not thou, frail man, that the Lord of heaven and earth doeth that which seemeth good unto him ?

26

" Lo ! many of the nations thou now seest suffering under the dragon, were worshippers of the first idol, which is called Licentiousness ; and until they shall by repentance and amendment of life, have expiated the crimes which they thereby committed, the sun of liberty which thou observedst to be nearly darkened in blood, shall not rise upon them, nor until then, shall their bonds be broken asunder.

27

Behold ! the hundred headed monster when let loose on the earth, was guilty of all manner of crime, cruelty, and oppression ; and shall not the dragon in like manner learn to catch his prey and feed in his turn, on the blood and vitals of the monster ?

CHAP. XIX.

The End of the Vision.

Now the angel, perceiving that my spirit was sore troubled and vexed within me at what I had beheld, took compassion upon me, and bade me turn mine eyes toward the west.

2

So I did as he spake, and behold my heart was cheered with a seemly prospect.

3

For lo ! in the midst of the ocean, I beheld a fair and beautiful island, on which the sun of freedom shone with exceeding brightness.

4

Her flowery meadows were inviting to the eye, and numerous herds and flocks were feeding on her verdant pastures.

5

Methought I heard the murmuring of her water brooks, and the sweet melody of the birds of her woods.

6

The shepherd leaning on his crook, stood musing on the face of the hill, tending his peaceful fold; and the husbandman was reaping in gladness the rich crop he had sown in the spring.

7

Now in the midst of the numerous herds in the island, I saw a sturdy bull with terrible horns, the guardian of the flock.

8

And the bull who roared and bellowed with mighty ire, stood on the sea shore, with his head turned towards the land of troubles, wherein the dragon prevailed.

9

And lo! I asked the angel whence arose the great fury of the bull?

10

And he spake, and said unto me, that the dragon which was on the opposite side of the sea, had often threatened the safety of the flock

and of the land; but that the bull terrified him,
and was ready to toss him and gore him to
death, if peradventure he came within his
reach.

11

Now the angel said, to the intent that I might
shew thee all these things art thou brought hi-
ther, go, therefore, and declare all that thou
hàst seen to the people of Albion.

12

And warn them against the perverse wickedness which brought upon the other nations of
the earth, the great and terrible calamities which
thou hast now beheld with thine eyes, and heard
with thine ears.

13

And behold! how glad was I when I awoke
and found myself in the peaceful and plentiful
land of my fathers !

14

Yea, that very land over which good king
Albanus reigns, whose throne is reared on love,
and not on terror; and around which there administer not blood-thirsty legions, but the holy keepers of the sacred records of religion, and

the guardians of the rights and privileges of the people; the learned in wisdom and in counsel, and in the laws of the land.

14

That land in which the law knoweth no distinction of rank, but is administered with impartial justice to the high and to the low, the rich and the poor, and in which every man is tried by his equals.

15

That land in which the voice of genuine freedom is triumphant.

16

In which the tongue of the senator is free even to abuse, and the pen of the writer with impunity inditeth scandalous things.

17

That land to which imprisonment and death are strangers, save where impartial justice, and venerable law inflict them on the guilty head.

18

That free and happy land, in which an hair of the head, or a morsel of bread, of the meanest of one of the people, cannot be injured even by the king on the throne!

19

Give not, then, grudgingly, O people of Albion, but with a willing heart, that which is necessary to maintain your happiness and greatness, and to protect you against the scourges of the tyrant Napoleon.

20

For in place of a part, he would take from you all that belongeth, and is dear unto you; and would moreover put your wives and your children to the sword, and cover the land wherein ye dwell with desolation and bloodshed.

CHAP. XX.

CHAP. XX.

The warnings and admonitions which the Angel gave in commission, to be delivered unto the King of Albion, and to his first born, and to all the sons and daughters of the King.—2. As also unto the Rulers and Counsellors of the land, and the Judges thereof, and unto all the people who dwell therein.

LISTEN then, and give ear, O people of Albion, to the warnings and admonitions which the angel of heaven gave in commission to be delivered unto you.

2

Beware, O Albions, of the worship of the first idol, which is called Licentiousness; because, on the day ye worship the same, ye shall surely perish.

3

And the wrath of the Lord shall be kindled against you, even unto your utter ruin and destruction.

4

For if it shall so happen, that ye listen unto

the deceits and seductions of the idol, and give yourselves up after the manner of the Gauls, unto sedition, conspiracy, and rebellion, treason, irreligion, and tumult, which are the fruits thereof; the same judgments shall visit you, which visited the land of Gaul, and fire and sword, rapine and murder, blood and famine, shall light upon the land.

5

And after the manner of the Gauls, and of the other nations above written, ye shall be delivered into the hands of the second idol, Napoleon, or of some such terrible scourge.

6

And ye shall be deprived of the great and invaluable blessings which you and your forefathers have enjoyed for many generations, as the reward of righteousness and of truth.

7

Furthermore, your lands shall be desolated and laid waste, and your silver and gold, and your corn, and your cattle, and your sheep, and whatsoever is precious unto you, shall be taken away.

H

8

Your cities, towns, and villages, shall be burnt and destroyed, and your sons and your daughters; yea, even your first born shall be led into captivity.

9

Ye shall be scourged, and ruled with a rod of iron, and all the threats and boastings of Napoleon, which it hath pleased the Lord for the present to turn far from you, shall be visited upon you, and your children's children, to the third and fourth generation.

10

For lo! the same God that hath delivered the other nations of the earth into the hands of the Tyrant, because of their unrighteousness, can do so unto you in like manner.

11

And the same God that hath given unto Napoleon the dominion over the land, can, in the fulness of his power, also give unto him the dominion over the mighty deep.

12

So that he may pass over the sea which divideth the land of Gaul from the land of Albion, with his warlike and numerous hosts, and overcome the people thereof, and slay them with great slaughter, and smite them from off the face of the earth.

. 13

Beware, therefore, O people of Albion, of the crafts and subtleties of the devil, who was heretofore in the form of the first idol, namely, Licentiousness, and now appeareth in the shape of Napoleon, the second idol of the Gauls.

14

For unto whom can this man be likened, but unto Satan, the enemy of mankind!

15

Continue, O good king Albanus! as heretofore, to fear God, and keep his commandments, and to walk humbly before the Lord thy God.

16

Let gentleness and mercy, peace and truth, piety and devotion, continue to mark thy paths, and make thee a bright and shining example of all manner of virtue unto the people, over whom the Lord hath appointed thee to reign in gladness and prosperity.

17

For by so doing, the people shall prosper in all manner of health and wealth; and when it shall please God to call thee, after having reigned for many years yet to come, from thine earthly kingdom, he will give unto thee a crown of glory, happiness, and immortality, in the kingdom of heaven, which knoweth no end, and is visited with no tribulation.

18

O prince! thou first born of good king Albanus, set before thee and follow the example of thy royal parent, and like him, fear God and keep his commandments.

19

So that the people over whom thou shalt peradventure rule, may, from a regard to thy person, and reverence for thy virtues, be in the hour of danger as a wall of defence round about thy throne, as in the time of the king thy father.

20

Be assured, O prince! that virtue and righteousness, are the firmest pillars of the throne, and of the state; and that without them there is neither happiness nor safety in earthly things.

21

For lo! even so it is, as written in this book, that all the kings and nations of the earth, who have fallen in these latter days, were estranged from God, and had become wicked in the imaginations of their hearts, and practices of their lives; so that it pleased the Lord to deliver them into the hands of their enemies, and to destroy them altogether.

22

But it hath hitherto seemed good unto the Almighty, to spare the nation over whom thou art destined peradventure to reign; because of the goodness of the king thy father, and of the people over whom he ruleth.

23

Take awful warning, therefore, from the fall of other princes; honour the king, and fear and obey the only true and living God, so that when thy royal father is called unto his heavenly kingdom, thou mayest reign in his stead for many days and years, over a free, loving, and happy people.

24

Then, when the evil day cometh, thou shalt not be afraid, and in the time of affliction, and at the hour of death, thou shalt be comforted, and supported by the spirit of God.

25

Now, O ye princes, and princesses of the land of Albion! as it hath pleased God to exalt you in rank, so may ye be eminent for virtue and piety.

26

Thereby affording comfort and happiness to your royal parents in the evening of their days; and to your inferiors a salutary example of all goodness and excellence.

27

Nor let it be said in ire, by the people who uphold you, that the grey hairs of your royal and beloved parents descend with sorrow to the grave, because of the sins and iniquities of their children.

CHAP. XXI.

Admonitions and Warnings to the Priests and Nobles of the land.—2. To the Representatives and Counsellors of the people.—3. To Judges and Magistrates.

O YE chief priests of the land and preachers of the gospel of truth! remember whose servants ye are; and while with your lips ye are proclaiming goodly instructions, and holy things, let your lives be patterns of all manner of virtue.

2

And thus give testimony to the excellency of the doctrines which ye preach and profess, as the ministers of a great and just God.

3

Banish far from you hypocrisy, worldly mindedness, licentiousness of life and doctrine, and all other unrighteousness.

4

While ye are administering spiritual and everlasting things, do not be constantly grasping at those which are temporal and perishing, and thereby manifesting too great a desire for the honours and enjoyments of this mortal life.

5

For whensoever ye act in this manner, ye belie the doctrines which ye preach, and are a reproach to the religion of Christ.

6

Remember, that unto you is committed the care and guidance of the souls of the people of this world, for which you must be one day accountable; and that your own souls are in the power of that great and pure Judge, at whose tribunal you must answer for your sacred charge with severe scrutiny, and stand or fall accordingly.

7

Ye nobles of the land! upon whom it hath pleased God to bestow honour, power, and wealth, let your rank be no less distinguished for its dignity, than for its goodness and virtue.

8

Command the respect and esteem of your inferiors, by eminent and conspicuous virtues and excellencies, and conciliate their love and affection by mercy, tenderness, and condescension.

9

In order thereto, be not strangers unto the people; but dwell in the mansions, and on the lands wherewith God blessed your noble fathers before you, and hath now blessed you; and be in the midst of your kinsmen and dependents, to comfort, and do them good.

10

For otherwise, if ye reside in great and corrupt cities, afar off from the people, and thus become estranged from them, how can they stand you in stead in the day of trouble and danger, as in the times of your fathers?

11

Then shall the land rejoice, and be glad of its nobles, and prosperity and security shall attend them; nor shall they be overthrown and destroyed, after the manner of those of the land of Gaul, and of the other nations of the earth, who were unmindful of these things, and consequently became the sport and derision of the multitude, who houted and trampled them under foot.

12

Ye representatives and counsellors of the people, and members of the great assembly of the nation! be exemplary, in like manner, for the purity and integrity of your conduct; fear God and honour the king!

13

Then shall your counsels prosper, and conduce to the good of the state; nor be like unto chaff, or the counsel of the ungodly, which is brought to nought, and driven to and fro.

14

Cease from all manner of wrangling, reviling, strife, and vain contention, which serve only to distract the measures of good king Albanus, at a time when nearly all the world have combined, and are waging cruel war against him, and threaten to destroy him and his people.

15

Unite with the king, your good and lawful governor, in heart and hand, and as one man, that the people may do so in like manner; lest the enemy, seeing a house divided against itself, rejoice, and say unto themselves; " Let us persevere, for we shall assuredly prevail in the end."

16

" For this people must fall into our hands because of their strife, and vain contentions in the hour of danger, and when the battle is at their gates."

17

Take warning, then, O great assembly of the nation! and let not contention, selfish considerations, and vain glory, harden your hearts, and darken your understandings, in the moment of mighty trouble and peril, while the land in which you dwell, and the king and people who put their trust in you, are beset on every side, and threatened with universal ruin and destruction.

18

O ye judges, and ministers of the laws of the land! be ye also conspicuous for all manner of purity, and rectitude of conduct; and let integrity and truth, justice and mercy, mark all your ways and judgments.

19

So that ye may be approved of men in this

world, and of God in the world to come, when
called upon to answer for your judgments on
earth, at a tribunal in heaven of infallible wisdom and justice.

20

Magistrates and inferior judges of the land!
hold fast your integrity and loyalty, and while
you are a pattern to the people in the purity
of your lives, keep them also in respectful
subordination and obedience to the laws; that
they may not violate the same, and like the
Gauls revel in all manner of iniquity and licentiousness, to their own bitter misery and
ruin.

21

O ye people of Albion! rich and poor, young
and old! hear what the warning voice of heaven hath to say unto you.

22

Whosoever it hath pleased God to bless in
his store, let him beware lest he forget who is
the Lord, and let him remember that his wealth
and riches are a sacred trust, placed in his
hands for the good and comfort of his less favoured, poor, and wretched fellow-creatures.

23

And for that trust he must render an account to him who gave it, at the final day of retribution, and according to the account which he rendereth, shall his doom be determined.

24

Whosoever it hath pleased God to afflict with poverty, " Let him beware lest he put forth his hand and steal."

25

Let him remember also that his afflictions are, as it were, but for a moment, and that true happiness is alone to be found in the heavenly mansions.

26

That the treasures of this life are fleeting and uncertain, and mixed with many alloys.

CHAP. XXII.

CHAP. XXII.

Admonitions to the Matrons and Daughters of Albion.

O YE matrons of Albion! shew unto the daughters thereof an example of prudence and propriety in speech, as well as in behaviour; and make home comfortable and inviting to your husbands.

2

Be careful of your domestic concerns, and avoid all revellings and gossipings at home or abroad, by night or by day.

3

Above all, be chaste and virtuous, and faithful to the marriage bed, employing yourselves chiefly, not in mirth, gaiety, and feasting; but in the care and education of your children, implanting in their tender minds the principles of virtue and religion.

4

For true it is, that upon the mother often depends the important trust of instilling into the minds of her children, those leading truths of religion and morality, which are to become the foundation of their individual excellence and happiness in life, and of their usefulness to their country.

5

And be assured, O mothers of families! that your duty in this respect is not less sacred than that of the ministers of our holy religion!

6

For while your husbands are engaged in their worldly avocations, to you is assigned the important task of laying the ground-work, on which the future superstructure of virtue must be raised.

7

Daughters of Albion! as ye are fair to look upon, so also be ye chaste, modest, and virtuous!

8

More careful and solicitous about the graces of the mind, than the ornaments of the person.

9

Cultivate and enrich your minds with every useful, amiable, and ornamental virtue.

10

Guard against the frivolities and absurdities of the frantic manners and fashions of the age in which ye live.

11

Let your attire be decent and becoming, neat and elegant; not too slender, expensive, or gaudy; but fitted for the land in which ye live, and proportioned to the means wherewith God hath blessed you.

12

Let not your eyes roam boldly on the faces of men, neither affect the coy air, nor assume the wanton gait.

13

But let your beauty shine, and your charms disclose themselves, in gentle and diffident deportment, and in the downcast look of virtuous modesty.

14

Train yourselves up to those virtues and accomplishments fitted to make you amiable mothers of children, so that the places of the departed matrons of the land may be properly supplied, and the young men thereof blessed with good wives.

15

Well knowest thou, O woman! the power and controul which thou possessest over the heart of man.

16

Thou canst either lead him by thy soft persuasions, to the holy altars of religion; correct his wandering and licentious thoughts, and animate him with the love of virtue and of glory!

17

Or thou canst by the same means call into action the vilest propensities of his nature, blow his passions into flame, and stir him up to treason and to crimes!

18

Use, therefore, thy influence discreetly, and to good account, inspiring the young men of the land with the love of their king and their country.

19

Stimulating them, moreover, to the defence thereof, that they may prove a safeguard

around thee, O fair one of Albion! and preserve thy person from the insult of a brutal
foe!

20

Heaven and victory forbid! that ever a hostile soldier should take a daughter of Albion by
the hand, or disturb the repose of her peaceful
fireside.

21

Heaven forbid! that ever a hostile soldier
should reap the rich crops, or eat the fair bread
of Albion!

22

Heaven and victory forbid! that ever an in-
vading foe should pollute the holy and sacred
altars of the land, or tread upon the revered
tombs of her departed fathers !

23

It is the recollection of thee, O woman! the
desire of obtaining thy admiration, and of se-
curing thy safety, that often animates the warrior in the direful conflict, and careless of danger, makes him pant for glory and for victory !

24

Noble and fascinating are thy attributes,

when governed by religion, patriotism, knowledge, and the gentler graces; but ah! how terrible when perverted and corrupted in their native and genuine sources; how ruinous to
mankind, and subversive of the social com-
pact!

25

Neither say, O woman! that too much is
herein ascribed to thy influence.

26

The tempting persuasions of Eve ended in
the fall of man, and the loss of paradise!

27

The infidelity of Helen proved the downfall
of Troy, and brought upon Greece a train of
innumerable ills!

28

The soothing blandishments of Cleopatra lost
the world to Mark Anthony!

CHAP. XXIII.

General Admonitions to the People of Albion.

O YE ancients of the land! let your grey hairs be unto you a crown of glory; and when your hoary heads descend into the grave, your souls shall ascend to heaven, and mingle with the spirits of the just!

2

Ye who rejoice in your youth, and the fulness of your strength! remember that disease, age, and death, are rapidly advancing.

3

Devote, therefore, the strength of your days to the practice of whatever is good and amiable, so that when the infirmities of nature shall overtake you, you may be found in the full possession of a virtuous and vigorous soul, and die the death of the righteous!

4

Parents! be careful to inculcate on the minds of your children the precepts of religion and morality, and exemplify the same in the purity and holiness of your own lives.

5

Children and little ones! obey the precepts and admonitions of your parents, fear God and honour the king!

6

So that if it shall please the Almighty to summon you hence, you may be reunited to those companions of your innocent years, who may have gone before you to the mansions of peace!

7

When, therefore, your spotless souls shall be required of you; may the whispering angel say; "Sister spirit, come away,"—"For of such is the kingdom of God!"

8

Masters! be gentle to, and reasonable with your servants, and inferiors, even as you expect the God of heaven to be merciful unto you.

9

Servants! see that ye be honest, faithful, and

obedient to your earthly master in all things, so that ye may be approven of by your heavenly master, and thereby receive at his hands, those wages which are kept in store for the humble heirs of immortality.

10

For when changed by death, ye shall experience none of the distinctions which God in his infinite wisdom has appointed to prevail in this lower world.

11

Then lo! a voice from heaven was heard, saying; " if the people of Albion shall listen unto these warnings and admonitions, the blessings which the only true and living God hath vouchsafed, shall be continued unto them, and to their children's children for generations yet unborn!"

12

" The land wherein they dwell shall bring forth her increase, and God, even their own God, shall give them his blessing!"

13

" The dominion over the sea, and health and wealth, and all manner of security and happiness shall moreover be continued unto the people thereof !"

14

" But if they shall, on the contrary, despise these warnings and admonitions, thousands and ten thousands of evils shall afflict the land; and the inhabitants thereof shall be delivered into the hands of their enemies."

15

" And all the judgments foretold and denounced in this book shall come upon the people, and scourge them; yea, even unto the excessive bitterness of their souls."

16

And when the voice had ceased speaking, the people marvelled within themselves and said, " yea, verily, these sayings are worthy of all acceptation !"

17

" Now, therefore, let us fear and worship the God of our fathers, and keep his commandments !"

18

" Moreover, let us serve, honour, and obey the

king whom the Lord hath appointed to rule over us in justice and mercy!"

19

And lo! an echo proceeding as it were from the mountains and the vallies, cried with a mighty voice—AMEN.

CONCLUSION.

CONCLUSION.

Thus endeth the First Book of Napoleon, the Tyrant of the Earth; and if it shall please God to prolong unto the Author thereof, the blessing of life, until the Tyrant is either slain by the glittering sword of man, or cut down by the sable scythe of death, a Second Volume shall then be written.

It is, however, devoutly to be wished, that the remainder of the Tyrant's days and deeds, may be comprised in a short and early epitaph.

Yet this man, amidst all his evils, has, through the wise ordination of Providence, been of use to the present generation, by counteracting the spirit of revolution, impatience of legitimate authority, and proneness to violent and dangerous changes.

He has moreover diverted to manly and warlike ends the overflowing wealth of Albion, wherewith she might otherwise have purchased her own ruin. By his menaces her young men have been awakened from the slumbers of luxurious sloth, and roused and inured to the art and toils of war, and thus has Albion become invincible, a terror to all her enemies, and to none more than to the Tyrant himself.

Now, may good king Albanus continue to reign for many days and years in health and wealth, and in the hearts of a brave, loyal, free, happy, and loving people, who never cease shouting all day long, " O King, live for ever !"

ELIAKIM.

END OF BOOK I.

Printed by John Moir, Royal Bank Close, Edinburgh.

Made in United States
Troutdale, OR
04/10/2024

19097456R00086